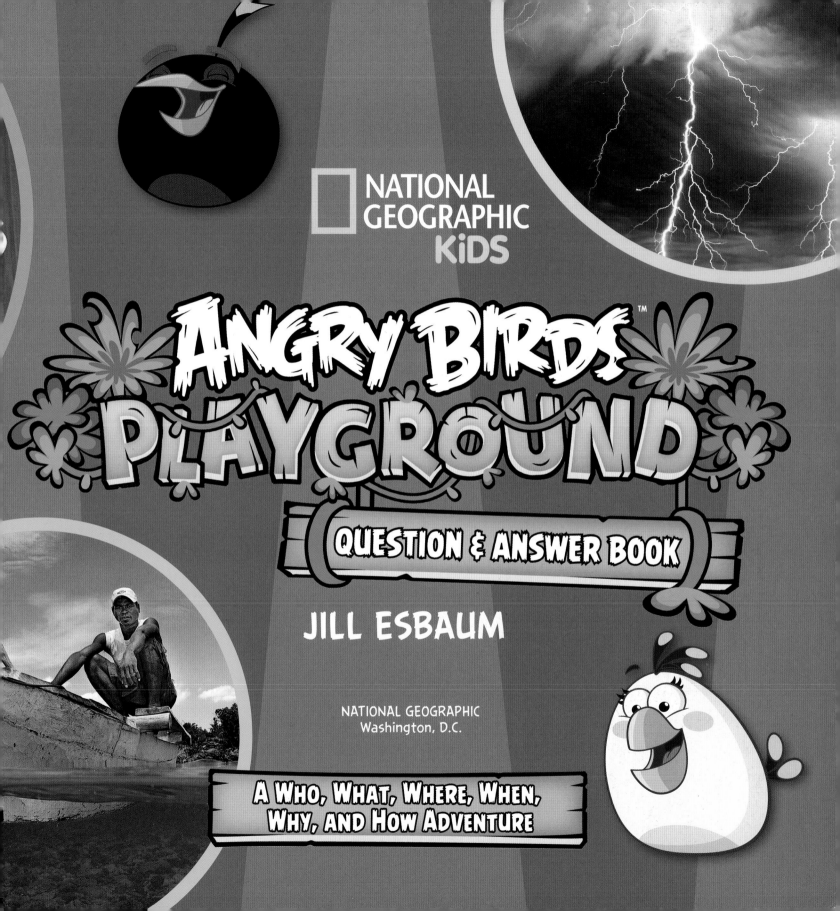

NATIONAL
GEOGRAPHIC
KiDS

ANGRY BIRDS™ PLAYGROUND

QUESTION & ANSWER BOOK

JILL ESBAUM

NATIONAL GEOGRAPHIC
Washington, D.C.

A WHO, WHAT, WHERE, WHEN, WHY, AND HOW ADVENTURE

For Collin, Carter, and McKinley

The National Geographic Society is one of the world's largest nonprofit scientific and educational organizations. Founded in 1888 to "increase and diffuse geographic knowledge," the Society's mission is to inspire people to care about the planet. It reaches more than 400 million people worldwide each month through its official journal, *National Geographic,* and other magazines; National Geographic Channel; television documentaries; music; radio; films; books; DVDs; maps; exhibitions; live events; school publishing programs; interactive media; and merchandise. National Geographic has funded more than 10,000 scientific research, conservation, and exploration projects and supports an education program promoting geographic literacy.

For more information, please visit nationalgeographic.com, call 1-800-NGS LINE (647-5463), or write to the following address:
National Geographic Society
1145 17th Street N.W.
Washington, D.C. 20036-4688 U.S.A.

Visit us online at nationalgeographic.com/books

For librarians and teachers: ngchildrensbooks.org

More for kids from National Geographic: kids.nationalgeographic.com

For information about special discounts for bulk purchases, please contact National Geographic Books Special Sales:
ngspecsales@ngs.org

For rights or permissions inquiries, please contact National Geographic Books Subsidiary Rights: ngbookrights@ngs.org

Library of Congress Cataloging-in-Publication Data

Esbaum, Jill.
  Angry birds playground : question and answer book : a who, what, where, when, why, and how adventure / by Jill Esbaum.
      pages cm
  Includes bibliographical references and index.
  ISBN 978-1-4263-1808-5 (hardcover : alk. paper) -- ISBN 978-1-4263-1809-2 (reinforced library binding : alk. paper)
  1. Children's questions and answers--Juvenile literature. I. Title.
      AG195.E825 2015
      002.083--dc23
      2014036173

Printed in Hong Kong
15/THK/1

Contents

PUZZLING PEOPLE 8

AMAZING ANIMALS 32

ASTOUNDING INVENTIONS 58

TERRIFIC TRAVEL 78

NUTS ABOUT NATURE 94

QUIZ TIME 116

BONUS ACTIVITIES 120

GLOSSARY 124

INDEX 126

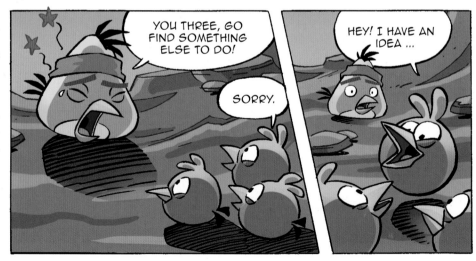

6

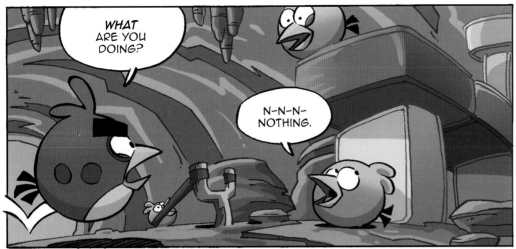

PUZZLING PEOPLE

FINISH

FIRST CATEGORY. GET READY, BIRDS!

No two people are exactly alike. They have different skin colors, personalities, faces, and bodies. Different likes and dislikes, talents, and problems. But people are alike in many ways, too...ways that might seem strange to animals.

WE'RE GOING TO FLY AWAY WITH THIS GAME!

◁ NUTS ABOUT NATURE

WHY DO PEOPLE WEAR CLOTHES?

Unlike animals, people don't have fur or feathers to protect them from the sun, wind, rain, and cold. So long ago they started wearing animal skins and furs to cover up.

Later, people learned how to weave fibers into cloth, then how to dye it different colors. Eventually, they learned how to cut and sew the cloth to make it fit a variety of body shapes—and modern clothes were born.

Now people wear clothing for lots of reasons. Some wear uniforms as part of their jobs, like baseball players, chefs, and police officers. Fancy clothes make celebrations and parties more festive, while costumes make holidays like Halloween more fun. And some people choose their clothes to express their own personal style!

FURRY FIRSTS!
Stone Age clothes were made of animal hides.

10

TOGA TIME!

When people first learned to weave fibers into cloth, they threw a long piece of it over one shoulder, then simply draped the rest around themselves and pinned it in place.

HOW DO YOU THINK I'D LOOK IN CLOTHES?

OVERDRESSED.

WHY IS HUMAN SKIN DIFFERENT COLORS?

It's all about melanin, a substance in people's skin that protects it from sunburn. Darker skin has more melanin, which means that person's ancestors lived in a sunny place. Lighter skin has less melanin, so that person's ancestors came from somewhere less sunny.

The less melanin people have protecting their skin, the easier they burn. The sun gives off invisible but powerful ultraviolet light. When lighter-skinned people are out in the sun too long, their skin burns, turning red and—ouch!—painful.

I'VE ALWAYS WISHED I WERE PURPLE.

SEEING SPOTS!
Freckles are clumps of melanin.

13

WHY DO SOME PEOPLE WEAR EYEGLASSES?

People wear glasses to see better—some to see far away, some to see close up. If the inside of a person's eyes aren't shaped a certain way, light doesn't go in perfectly. That makes eyesight fuzzy. Curved lenses—glasses—can correct the way light goes into the eye and sharpen a person's vision.

YO, CHECK ME OUT.

NICE SHADES!

Sunglasses cut the sun's brightness, so wearing them makes people more comfortable when they're outdoors on sunny days. Some glasses also protect eyes from the sun's harmful ultraviolet rays. And some people wear sunglasses to look cool.

WHY DO PEOPLE WEAR JEWELRY?

People wear jewelry to decorate themselves. Ancient people started adorning themselves by winding feathers into their hair. They strung shells or stones or wood or bones to wear around their necks (necklaces), arms (bracelets), or through their earlobes (earrings). As time went on, people started to make fancier pieces, using precious metals, like silver and gold, and precious stones, like diamonds and rubies.

Now wearing jewelry has a lot of different purposes. It can be fun, fancy, and meaningful. Some people exchange rings when they wed to symbolize their marriage. Jewelry can also show power: Golden crowns have sat on the heads of many leaders, from the pharaohs of ancient Egypt to Queen Elizabeth II of today's Great Britain.

FIT FOR A QUEEN!

The Imperial State Crown of England is studded with 2,868 diamonds, 17 sapphires, and 11 emeralds.

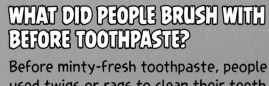

WHY DO PEOPLE'S BABY TEETH FALL OUT?

A kid-size mouth has room for 20 small teeth. But as our bodies grow bigger, so do our mouths. As that happens, bigger, stronger teeth push out the baby teeth and grow in to take their place.

Brushing washes away bacteria that sticks to teeth and causes holes called cavities. Those can hurt!

WHAT DID PEOPLE BRUSH WITH BEFORE TOOTHPASTE?

Before minty-fresh toothpaste, people used twigs or rags to clean their teeth with things like ashes, brick dust, ground-up chalk, or even smashed charcoal. They didn't swallow.

I BRUSH WITH A TWIG FROM MY NEST!

18

WHAT MAKES A BURP?

People swallow air when they eat and drink. That air builds up in their stomachs until it has to escape. Some foods—or an upset stomach—set off burps, too.

WHY DO PEOPLE GET HICCUPS?

Hiccups often happen when people eat too fast or too much. Feeling nervous or excited can cause them, too, or if a stomach or throat is irritated.

It all starts with the diaphragm (DIE-uh-fram), a muscle between the chest and stomach that helps people breathe. Breathe in, and the diaphragm pulls down to help pull air into the lungs. Breathe out, and the diaphragm relaxes. When the diaphragm is irritated it jerks down quickly, and air is sucked into the throat suddenly. Located in the throat is a person's voice box, and when that little gush of air hits it, *hic-hic-hic.*

MEOW-HIC!
Even cats and rats are known to get hiccups!

HICCUPS MUST FEEL LIKE LITTLE EARTHQUAKES.

21

WHY DO PEOPLE LIVE IN DIFFERENT KINDS OF HOMES?

People started building homes for safety. They needed protection from the weather and from wild animals. Ancient peoples began building different kinds of dwellings to provide all these things, and people have never stopped creating new kinds of places to live their lives.

Today, the kind of building a person lives in depends on where they live and what they like. Many people live in houses made from some combination of wood, brick, stone, concrete, and glass. In big cities, people live in tall skyscrapers filled with apartments. In rural areas, people may live in grass huts, tents, clay domes, or simple tin structures. No matter what kind of building, they're all home.

MONGOLIAN YURT

THERE'S NO PLACE LIKE HOME!

22

FROM THE GROUND UP!

Some people build their homes with cob, a substance made of mud mixed with straw. How do they mix the two? By stomping the straw into the mud with their feet.

ENGLISH COB HOUSE

GERMAN CASTLE

HONG KONG APARTMENT BUILDINGS

23

WHY CAN'T PEOPLE FLY?

Our skeleton is designed for walking, not flying. Our feet have 26 bones each! And people bones are filled with marrow—soft, spongy stuff where blood cells are made.

But every part of a bird's skeleton is designed to help it fly. Many of a bird's bones are hollow, filled with nothing but air. That makes them lighter. Even their tailbones have a special job. They support feathers that birds can move while flying to change direction quickly.

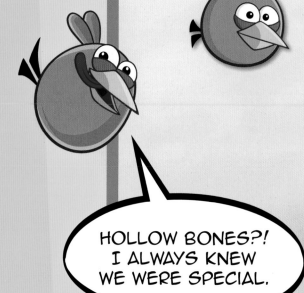

HOLLOW BONES?! I ALWAYS KNEW WE WERE SPECIAL.

HEAVY FEATHERS

The feathers of most birds weigh more than their skeletons.

OWIE

The bone kids break most often? The collarbone.

YOU CAN SAY THAT AGAIN!

25

YOUNGER AND FASTER

Children's nails grow faster than adults'.

HOW DO FINGERNAILS GROW?

Q&A

Fingernails and toenails are made of a type of protein called keratin. They are embedded into special, stretchy skin that sticks to the nails and holds them in place. When keratin cells gather just under the skin at the base of the nail, they push the nail up and out. Nails grow!

TOES ARE TOO CUTE TO BE CALLED "PIGGIES"!

FASTER THAN A SPEEDING FINGERNAIL!

Fingernails grow three to four times faster than toenails.

WHY DO PEOPLE MAKE MUSIC?

Most people would say that music just makes them feel good. For some, that "feel good" music is slow and soft. Others like the throb of rock tunes or the swinging rhythms of jazz. Or rap, with its steady, pulsing beat.

Scientists have proved that music really does affect people's emotions. The right melodies—with words or without—can bring tears to people's eyes or give them goose bumps. Speed up or slow down their heartbeat. Make them feel relaxed or even make them so happy they want—no, *need*—to dance.

STRIKE UP THE BAND!

THE MIGHTY MINI

Best-selling musical instrument in the world? The harmonica.

28

HUNGRY HEADBANGERS

Studies show that termites eat wood twice as fast if heavy metal music is being played nearby.

LOOKS LIKE A GOOD STORY!

YES, I REMEMBER THAT

Studies have shown that reading regularly improves a person's memory.

WHY DO PEOPLE READ AND WRITE?

People read and write to communicate so they can make sense of the world. Without language, life would be nearly impossible. Grown-ups couldn't drive if they couldn't follow signs. They couldn't apply for jobs or find out what's in their food or even follow directions to a place they needed to go. Reading improves people's imaginations and helps them become smarter.

But reading is FUN, too. It introduces people to new places, new experiences, new ideas, and new stories. A good book can help people discover who they are and what they stand for. Reading opens doors and hearts and minds.

TICKTOCK

After only six minutes of reading, a stressed person feels more relaxed.

Q&A AMAZING ANIMALS

FINISH ▷

THE NEXT CATEGORY IS ANIMALS.

Animals may be short, like spiders, or tall, like giraffes. As noisy as trumpeting elephants or as silent as fireflies. As furry as bears—or covered in feathers, beak to tail. Each kind of animal has habits and behaviors all its own.

ARE WE ANIMALS?

AMAZING
ANIMALS ▶

ASTOUNDING
INVENTIONS
▽

◀ TERRIFIC
TRAVEL

WHY ARE SOME BABY BIRDS BORN NAKED AND OTHERS WITH FEATHERS?

The word for birds born looking naked, or without feathers, is altricial (al-TRISH-ul). Altricial babies are helpless and need their parents to feed and care for them. They are usually born in nests not easily reached by predators, so it's okay if it takes them a while to grow up.

The word for birds born with feathers is precocial (pre-CO-shul). Precocial babies can run around and eat on their own soon after breaking out of their shells. That's good, because their nests are usually on or near the ground, easily reached by predators.

NO FEATHERS? HEE-HEE!

ALTRICIAL ROBIN CHICKS

PIGS WOULDN'T EVEN SEE THOSE TEENY EGGS!

WHO LAYS THE SMALLEST EGGS?

Hummingbirds. A Jamaican hummingbird, the vervain, has tiny eggs less than half an inch (1 cm) long.

WHO LAYS EGGS BESIDES BIRDS?

Fish, amphibians, reptiles, and most insects and spiders lay eggs. Only two mammals lay eggs, the platypus and the echidna (ih-KID-nuh).

The yellow inside an egg is the yolk. In fertilized eggs (the ones meant to grow young) the yolk feed the tiny embryo inside. (Don't worry. Eggs found in grocery stores are not fertilized.)

WELCOME TO THE WORLD, LITTLE GATOR!

PLATYPUS

HER ONE AND ONLY

Echidna moms lay only one leathery egg each year. The baby that hatches from this grape-size shell is called a puggle.

ECHIDNA? SOUNDS LIKE A SNEEZE.

HATCHING BABY ALLIGATOR

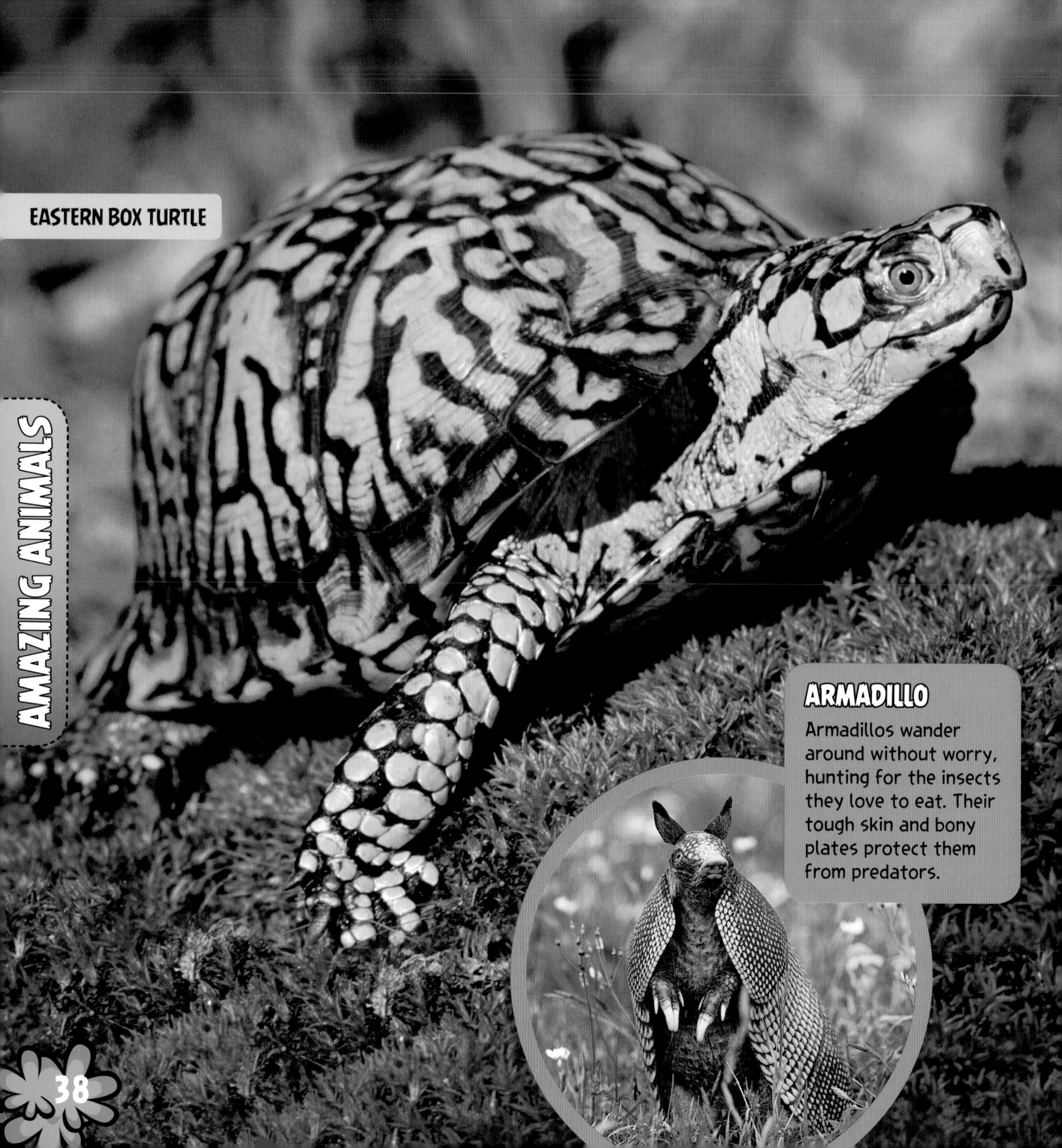

AMAZING ANIMALS

ARMADILLO

Armadillos wander around without worry, hunting for the insects they love to eat. Their tough skin and bony plates protect them from predators.

38

WHY DO TURTLES HAVE SHELLS?

Most turtles move slowly and their bodies are soft. Without their hard shells, predators would eat them! With their hard shells, they're safe.

Other animals, like porcupines and armadillos, have body parts that protect them too!

LET'S TAKE SOME OF THOSE QUILLS HOME ...

PORCUPINE

Normally, a porcupine's quills lie almost flat ... but when it is in danger–**BOING!**–they stand on end.

... TO POKE PIGS!

WHY DO FIREFLIES LIGHT UP?

Fireflies—or lightning bugs, as some people call them—have a spot under their abdomens where they make a chemical called luciferin. When air hits luciferin, it glows. A firefly can control how much air gets in, making its light flash on/off, on/off.

A firefly's glow attracts mates. It may also be a signal to predators—birds and spiders and frogs—that it doesn't taste good. But some frogs eat fireflies anyway, and then something weird happens: The frogs start glowing.

IF I EAT A FIREFLY, WILL MY TUMMY GLOW?

BUT, BOMB, YOU'RE NOT A FROG!

LIGHT UP!

Each of the 2,000 species of firefly has its **OWN FLASH PATTERN.**

41

KEEP GOING, SPIDEY. YOU CAN DO IT!

SPINY SPIDER

HOW LONG DOES IT TAKE TO SPIN A WEB?

That depends on the size of the web and the type of spider. Usually, a spider gets the job done in an hour or less.

42

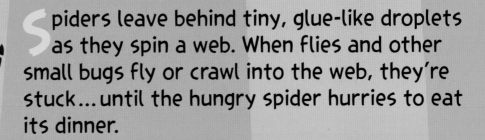

WHY ARE SPIDER-WEBS STICKY?

ARE SPIDERWEBS STRONG ENOUGH TO TRAP PIGS?

Spiders leave behind tiny, glue-like droplets as they spin a web. When flies and other small bugs fly or crawl into the web, they're stuck...until the hungry spider hurries to eat its dinner.

To keep from sticking to their own webs, spiders are careful to spin out some nonsticky strands. These are the only ones the spider steps on. They are also careful to walk lightly. Sometimes, only the teeny hairs on a spider's legs touch the web.

WASP SPIDER

WHY DO SPIDERS SPIN WEBS WHERE THEY DO?

Spiders make their webs where they think they'll catch the most flying or crawling bugs.

43

WHY DO CATS COUGH UP HAIR BALLS?

AMAZING ANIMALS

Cats like to stay clean, and the way they do that is to lick themselves. They can't help but swallow a little fur. The fur can form a ball in a cat's belly, and sooner or later, it has to come out. Or, you know, UP. *Blahhhk.*

YUCK.

DO CATS ALWAYS LAND ON THEIR FEET?

Most of the time they do. Cats possess a special reflex that allows them to rotate their bodies right side up to land on their feet.

HOW DO CATS PURR?

It's all about the throat. Scientists think purrs are made when muscles near a cat's vocal cords relax. As the cat breathes in and out, air hits the vibrating muscles, and... *PURRRRR.*

HEY, MR. ELEPHANT... WANNA GO HOME WITH ME AND STOMP SOME PIGS?

ELEPHANTS TALK TO EACH OTHER...

by smelling, touching, even using their own kind of sign language. Elephants can be **LOUD,** but they can also hear each other's low rumbles over long distances.

WHY DO ELEPHANTS HAVE SUCH FUNNY NOSES?

Those are called trunks, and they aren't funny to elephants. They're terrific tools! Elephants can suck water up their trunks to take a drink or cool off. They can suck dust, too, then blow it over their backs to keep away bugs. Fingerlike bumps at the end of the trunk can grab food, grasses, or tree branches.

ELEPHANTS LIVE IN FAMILY GROUPS.

Older females are tops in elephant families. Daughters always stick close to their mothers. Males leave the family to hang out with other males.

47

WHY DO BEARS SLEEP ALL WINTER?

Bears can't get the food they need to eat—nuts and berries—in winter. So each autumn, they eat as much as possible to build up their body fat. Then, around October, they look for a cave or hollow tree, curl up, and sleep away the winter, or hibernate.

During hibernation, all that extra fat keeps the bear alive. Its heartbeat drops to only ten beats per minute, and its body temperature drops, too. In April or May, the bear wakes up to a forest filled with spring treats.

BAT

CHIPMUNK

WHAT OTHER ANIMALS HIBERNATE?

Bats, marmots, rodents, such as chipmunks and woodchucks, and amphibians and reptiles, like frogs and snakes, to name just a few.

BLACK BEARS

49

WHY DO GIRAFFES HAVE LONG NECKS?

Giraffes spend most of the day eating leaves, especially those found at the top of the acacia tree. Without their long necks, giraffes couldn't eat their favorite food.

HEAVY LIFTING:

A giraffe's neck weighs as much as **600 POUNDS** (272 kg)**!**

HAPPY LANDINGS:

When a baby giraffe is born, it falls on its head—**THUMP!** But in less than one hour, the calf is up and ready to run.

51

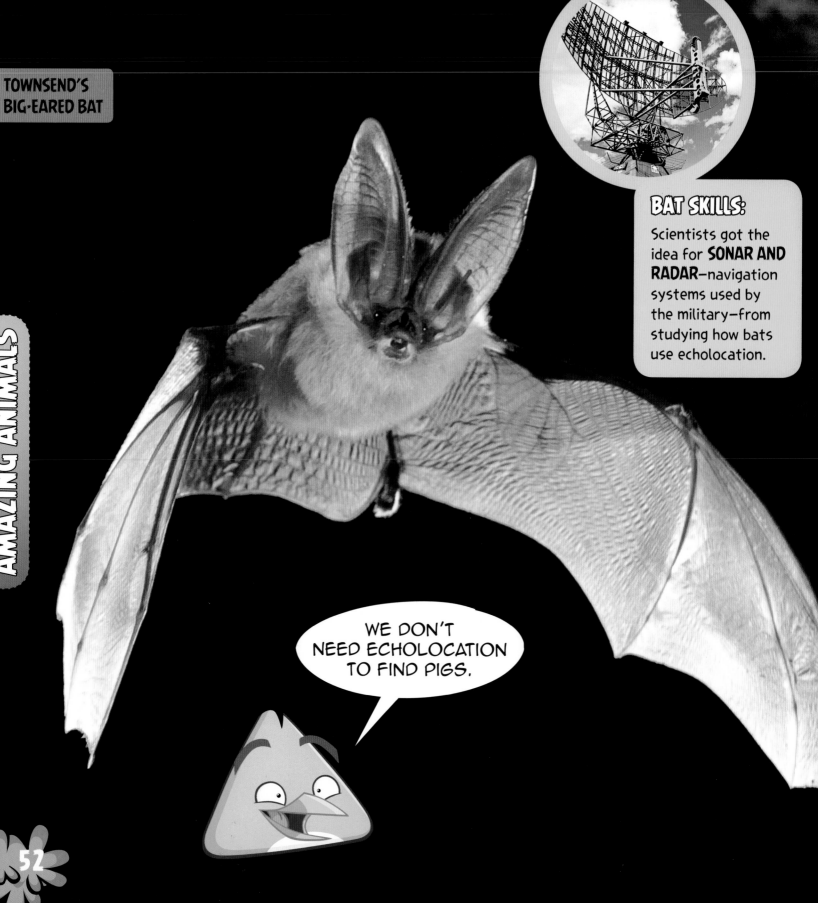

AMAZING ANIMALS

BAT SKILLS:
Scientists got the idea for **SONAR AND RADAR**–navigation systems used by the military—from studying how bats use echolocation.

WE DON'T NEED ECHOLOCATION TO FIND PIGS.

52

How do BATS SEE IN THE DARK?

Q&A

Have you ever shouted "HELLO" across a canyon or at a faraway wall and heard your own voice bounce back? That sound is sort of how bats "see" where objects are in the dark. To find their prey—flying insects—bats send out a high-pitched sound through their noses or mouths, then listen carefully. The way the sound bounces back tells them exactly where a bug is. This is called echolocation (eck-o-low-KAY-shun).

YEAH, WE CAN SMELL 'EM! P.U.!

BOTTLENOSE DOLPHIN

SHREW

HEARING THINGS:

Some other animals that use **ECHOLOCATION** are toothed whales, bottlenose dolphins, some birds, and shrews.

WHY ARE SOME ANIMALS BRIGHTLY COLORED AND OTHERS DULL?

Camouflage—the way an animal's skin, fur, or feathers blends into its surroundings—helps it survive. How? By making it almost invisible to other animals. Some animals use camouflage to hide from hunters. And predators can better stalk their prey if they go undetected.

Brightly colored animals aren't so great at hiding, but their markings also help them to survive. Those bright colors warn predators: "Don't eat me. I'm poisonous!" or "Watch out! I sting!"

NOW YOU SEE ME...

Predators, such as tigers, have excellent camouflage to help them **SNEAK UP** on their prey. Hey, everybody needs to eat!

WHICH ANIMAL IS SMARTEST?

Some scientists say the chimpanzee is the smartest animal. Others argue for the orangutan or the gorilla. Other smarty-pants animals? Bottlenose dolphins, pigs, parrots, whales, elephants, octopuses, squirrels, dogs, and crows.

HA! I KNEW THERE HAD TO BE BIRDS IN THERE!

WHICH ANIMAL IS THE FASTEST?

On land, that would be the cheetah, which can run 70 miles an hour (113 km/h). **BUT, WAIT!** A hooked black marlin (fish) has been recorded swimming at 82 miles an hour (132 km/h).

WHICH ANIMAL IS THE BIGGEST?

The biggest animal in the world is the blue whale, which can be 75 to 100 feet (23 to 30.5 m) long. Its **TONGUE** is the **SIZE OF AN ELEPHANT!**

57

Q&A ASTOUNDING INVENTIONS

YOU GUYS ARE GOING TO NEED AN INVENTION TO HELP YOU WIN!

People invent things for many reasons. To make their work easier. To make life better for others. To learn new things. Or simply for the joy of using their imagination and creativity.

WHEN WERE CRAYONS INVENTED?

The first coloring sticks were used in Europe, probably in the 1600s. They were made by mixing charcoal and oil, then rolling the mess into sticks. Later, somebody tried replacing the charcoal with colored powder. Later still, some inventive person discovered that mixing the powders with wax made a much sturdier coloring stick.

Today machines push warm, colored wax through small holes to form sticks of color, and another machine wraps each cooled crayon in paper.

MY FAVORITE IS YELLOW!

AND THE WINNER IS...

In 1993, Crayola users voted for their favorite color. The winner? Blue.

GETTING DIRTY!
Prehistoric artists made pictures using earth-toned clumps of chalk and clay.

CAVE PAINTINGS

WHO MADE THE FIRST MICROSCOPE?

The modern microscope was invented more than 400 years ago by a Dutchman named Zacharias Jansen, who usually made eyeglasses. It wasn't very powerful. Things only looked about 9x, or nine times, bigger than they really were.

A microscope's mirrors, lights, and curved lenses bend an object's reflection and magnify it (make it look much bigger). Scientists, doctors, and others use microscopes to help them learn. They can study tiny organisms that make people sick. They can test water to make sure it's clean enough to drink. They can see what minerals rocks are made of— and lots, LOTS more!

SEE ANY ANGRY BIRDS IN SPACE?

TO INFINITY AND BEYOND!
Telescopes use mirrors and lights and curved lenses in ways that help scientists see deep into space.

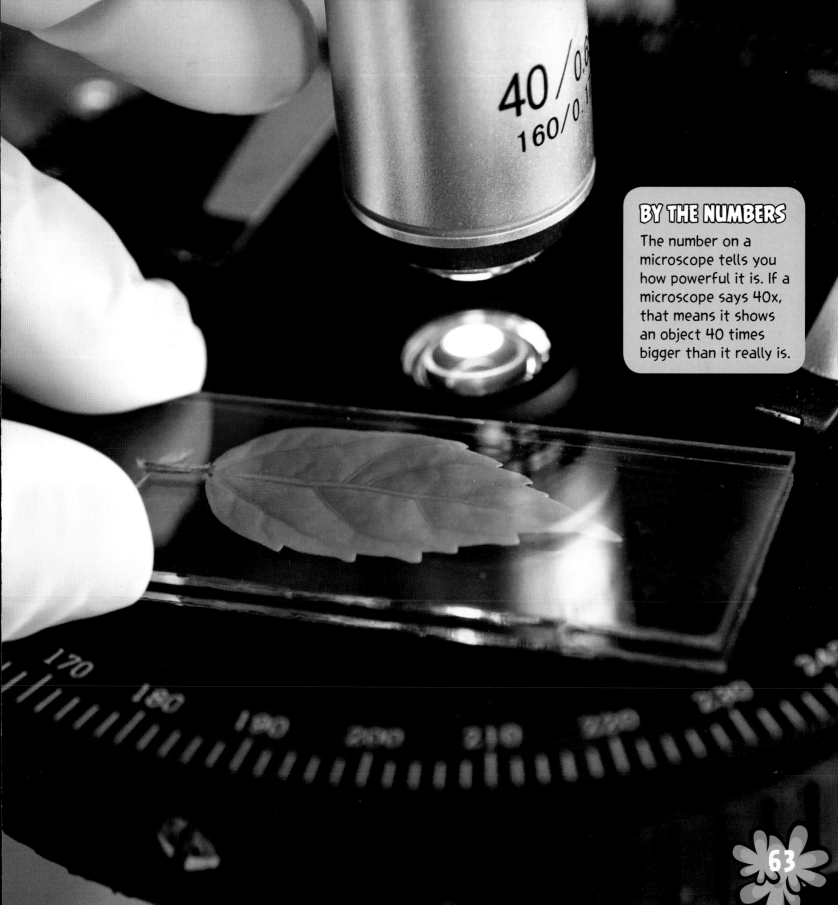

40 / 0.6
160/0.1

BY THE NUMBERS

The number on a microscope tells you how powerful it is. If a microscope says 40x, that means it shows an object 40 times bigger than it really is.

170   180   190   200   210   220

63

GASSY GLOBES

Small balloons that float in the air are filled with a special lighter-than-air gas called helium.

A ROOSTER FLEW IN THE FIRST BALLOON?

HE COCK-A-DOODLE-DID!

WHO INVENTED THE HOT-AIR BALLOON?

In 1783, French brothers Joseph-Michel and Jacques-Étienne Montgolfier designed a hot-air balloon they were sure could lift humans off the ground. Just to be on the safe side, they first sent up a sheep, a duck, and a rooster. The animals floated in the sky before they crashed to the ground. Alive! A few months later, the brothers sent up their friend Jean-François Pilâtre de Rozier, the first human to ride in a hot-air balloon.

Early hot-air balloons were made of silk, which tore easily and was hard to repair. Now most are made of lightweight, strong, sturdy nylon. Giant balloons are powered by flame-heated air. Because hot air is lighter than cold air, the balloon goes up, up, up.

MONTGOLFIER BALLOON

AN ANCIENT EGYPTIAN PAINTING
OF A QUEEN PLAYING SENET

PLAY NICE

Another early board game,
The Mansion of Happiness,
went on sale in 1843. Its
purpose was to teach children
how to behave properly.

WHAT WAS THE FIRST BOARD GAME?

TRAVEL GAMES

The first board game sold in America, way back in 1822, was called the **Traveller's Tour Through the United States.**

Nobody is absolutely sure. One game, called **Senet,** has been found in 5,000-year-old Egyptian burial chambers. **Chess** was played in Persia (now Iran) and India about 4,000 years ago. **Checkers** has also been around a long time—at least 3,500 years. And the modern game of **backgammon** has been enjoyed for more than 2,000 years.

WANNA PLAY CHECKERS? I'LL BE RED!

I'LL BE BLACK!

WHEN WERE ELEVATORS INVENTED?

The first elevator is believed to have been built by a Greek inventor named Archimedes more than 2,000 years ago. Early elevators were lifted or lowered using people, animals, or waterwheel power, but today there are two kinds of elevators, traction and hydraulic.

In traction elevators, a cable passes over a wheel. A powerful motor turns the wheel, pulling the cable, which lifts the elevator.

Hydraulic elevators move more slowly and are sometimes used in shorter buildings. In this type of elevator, a motor controls a giant piston that pushes the elevator up or lets it down carefully.

16TH-CENTURY MINE ELEVATOR

GOING UP!

IT HAS ITS UPS AND DOWNS.

The boxy space in which the elevator goes up and down is called the shaft.

69

HOW DOES A TV WORK?

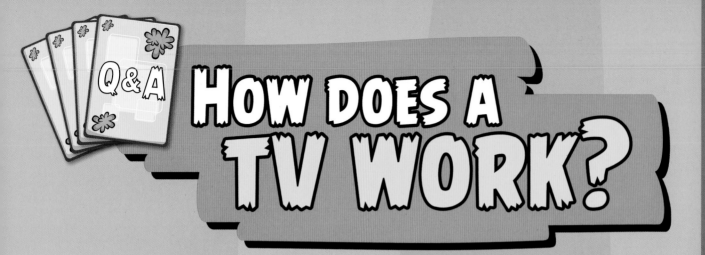

A TV camera changes images (pictures) to electrical impulses (signals). These signals are sent out along cables, or by radio waves, or from tall towers to satellites in space. Satellites gather the signals and reflect them back to Earth or on to another satellite. The signals are beamed back to Earth and caught by dish antennas, which send them on to people's televisions.

A TV has lines—tiny dots of light—across its screen, called pixels. These pixels flash color—red, blue, or green—the way the signal tells them to. Pixels change color superfast, making the picture appear to move on the screen.

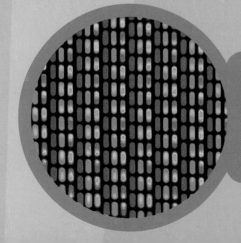

DOT TO DOT

The more pixels on a screen, the shar the picture. Get close enough to a TV and you'll be able to see the tiny pixe dots and watch them change color.

70

WHERE DID ELECTRIC GUITARS COME FROM?

Q&A

Stringed instruments have been around for thousands of years. But it wasn't until the 1920s that a Swiss-American named Adolph Rickenbacker figured out how to use electricity to amplify a guitar's sound (make it LOUDER). Now, musicians use electric guitars to play every type of music from rock and country to jazz and blues.

COOL KEYBOARD

A keytar is an electric piano that's slung around the neck and shoulders, like a guitar.

HIGHS AND LOWS

As a guitar player's fingers move up the neck of a guitar, the notes sound higher.

73

WHAT WAS THE FIRST VIDEO GAME?

The first video game, *Tennis for Two,* was invented in 1958 by a scientist named William Higinbotham. To play, two people with electronic controllers sent a bright dot bouncing back and forth across a tiny round screen. In the 1970s, the popularity of electronic games soared. Game consoles were everywhere—in gas stations and hotel lobbies, in amusement parks and restaurants. For 25 cents, anybody could play games like *Periscope, Killer Shark, Pong,* and *Space Invaders.* Today people can play video games almost anywhere—in their homes, on their computers, and even on their cell phones.

BEEP-BEEP!
Sound effects in the first video games were simple combinations of dings and beeps and bloops.

1970s ARCADE GAME

SPACE INVADERS

74

PONG VIDEO GAME

HELLO? CAN YOU HEAR ME NOW?

MARTIN COOPER, INVENTOR OF THE CELL PHONE

WHO INVENTED CELL PHONES?

An American, Martin Cooper, invented the first handheld cell phone in 1973. The thing was ten inches (25 cm) long and weighed as much as a medium-size cantaloupe. Its nickname? The Brick. The first time Cooper used the phone outdoors, in public, was in New York City. People gaped at him, he said. They were astounded that he could walk down the street while making a phone call.

BEAM ME UP!

In an interview, Martin Cooper said that he was inspired to invent the cell phone by the 1960s TV show *Star Trek* and Captain Kirk's small, handheld Communicator.

77

Q&A

TERRIFIC TRAVEL

FINISH ►

C'MON, MATILDA! ANOTHER CATEGORY FOR US TO DOMINATE!

People travel from place to place in many different types of vehicles. We use cars and trucks, buses and trains, boats and planes...even space labs! Each type of vehicle was created for a special purpose, whether it moves us along on a highway, on rails, or through water or sky.

◄ NUTS ABOUT NATURE

WHY ARE SCHOOL BUSES YELLOW?

TERRIFIC TRAVEL

It's all about safety. School buses have to be seen by other drivers, and seen quickly. Scientific tests showed that a bright yellow-orange color got people's attention faster than any other, even in rainy or foggy weather—even when it wasn't directly in front of people, but in their peripheral vision—over to one side or the other.

WHAT DID THE SCHOOL BUS DRIVER SAY TO THE FROG?

GIDDYUP!

Before school buses, city children got to distant schools in trucks or horse-drawn wagons. Country students walked or rode a horse or went by horse-drawn wagon.

81

WHY DOES A BOAT FLOAT?

YEAH. THE WATER IN THAT PUDDLE MUST NOT HAVE BEEN DEEP ENOUGH.

Buoyancy, the ability of an object to float in water, is what allows ships to float. Water moves aside to make room for whatever is put into it. That's called displacement. A ship is heavy! But the water it displaces is heavier yet. All that water pushes up and against the ship and keeps it afloat.

A boat's shape matters, too. When weight is spread out over a large area, there is more water underneath to push it up.

NOW THAT'S A BIG BOAT!

The *Allure of the Seas* is the longest cruise ship in the world. It is 1,187 feet (362 m) long. That's nearly the length of four football fields!

How do TRAINS work?

The first trains, invented in the late 1700s, were steam powered. Coal or wood was shoveled into a locomotive's firebox, burning hot enough to turn water to steam. The high-pressure steam traveled through pipes that, when opened, moved the heavy pistons connected to the drive wheels, which made those turn, and...*chug-a-chug-a, chug-a-chug-a!* These days, most locomotives run on diesel fuel or electricity. Electric locomotives are powered by overhead wires, or by a rail different from the ones their wheels roll on, or by battery.

CHOO-CHOO!

If you see smoke rising from the chimney of a train, you know it's a steam train. The smoke is from the fuel—wood or coal—burning in the train's firebox to keep it chugging along.

QUICK, COUNT THE CARS!

ZIP-ZOOM!

The speediest train is China's *Shanghai Maglev*. This train holds a record for whizzing along at 311 miles an hour (500 km/h)!

ELECTRIC CAR

WHAT MAKES A CAR GO?

Q&A

Cars get their power from the energy that fuels them—gas, electricity, or a combination of both.

A gas engine has a battery. The battery provides a spark that makes gas and air burn inside the engine, sort of like mini-explosions. These explosions give off energy. Another part of a car, the transmission, sends the energy from the engine to the wheels.

An electric car has an engine, too. But it's powered by rechargeable batteries. A controller sends electricity to the motor.

HOLD ON TIGHT!

Henry Ford's gas-powered Model T, introduced in 1908, was the first car driven by ordinary Americans. It sputtered along at top speeds of 40 to 45 miles an hour (64 to 72 km/h).

87

Q&A

HOW DOES A HELICOPTER STAY UP IN THE AIR?

TERRIFIC TRAVEL

Helicopters have two sets of rotor blades. The main blades—the ones on top—spin fast enough to lift the helicopter off the ground. The smaller tail rotor works *against* the force made by the main rotor blades. Used together, along with changing the angle of the blades, a pilot can make a helicopter go up and down, right and left, backward and forward, or hover in one spot. Heavier helicopters—and helicopters that need to lift heavy loads—need more than one main rotor blade.

FAST FLIGHTS

Helicopters are great when somebody needs to go a short distance in a hurry. They're used by hospital and police emergency teams, politicians, search and rescue squads, and even reporters checking out traffic snarls.

88

FLUPPITY-FLUPPITY-FLUPPITY!
Helicopters might also be called choppers, copters, helos, or whirlybirds.

BIG WUP. NOTHING BIRDS CAN'T DO.

AIRLINE EATS!

Most airline pilots and copilots eat different meals before and during a flight. That way, if food makes one sick, the other can still fly the plane.

WHERE IS THE WORLD'S BUSIEST AIRPORT?

Atlanta, Georgia, U.S.A.

WHY DON'T AIRPLANES FLAP THEIR WINGS?

Wings don't need to move. As an airplane cuts through the sky, air drags against it, slowing it down. All that moving air hits the wings, too. Wings are designed so that some air flows above them, but more air flows underneath. That air pushes up on the wings, lifting the plane. Adjusting small flaps on each wing helps airplanes lift higher or slow down.

WING FLAPS

WHY DON'T THEY JUST USE SLINGSHOTS TO FLY? EASY PEASY!

91

WHAT IS THE INTERNATIONAL SPACE STATION?

The International Space Station (ISS) is a science laboratory that orbits more than 200 miles (322 km) above Earth. Too big to be launched into space all at once, its sections were built here on Earth, then sent up to be joined together by astronauts. Begun in 1998 and finished in 2011, the space station is the size of a football field and as heavy as 37 school buses!

ANIMALS IN SPACE? LET'S GO!

WHAT ANIMALS FIRST WENT INTO SPACE?

Fruit flies. Scientists used them to test the safety of spaceflight. The flies made it back to Earth alive, paving the way for bigger animals like mice, monkeys, and dogs.

92

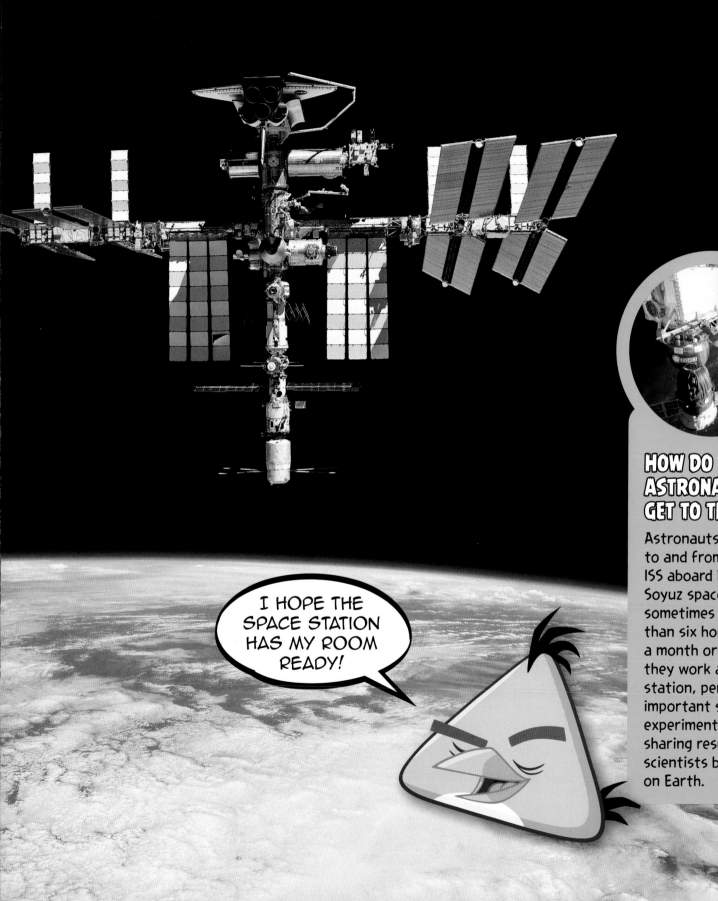

I HOPE THE SPACE STATION HAS MY ROOM READY!

HOW DO ASTRONAUTS GET TO THE ISS?

Astronauts rocket to and from the ISS aboard Russia's Soyuz spacecraft, sometimes in less than six hours. For a month or two, they work at the station, performing important science experiments and sharing results with scientists back here on Earth.

Q&A

NUTS ABOUT NATURE

FINISH

ALL RIGHT, BIRDS. IT'S THE LAST CATEGORY.

Trees and grass, sky and stars, mountains and seas. Nature is all around us. It is as gentle as a rainbow or as violent as an earthquake. It is as silent as a sprouting seed or as loud as too-close, cover-your-ears THUNDERBOOMERS.

WHY IS GRASS GREEN?

Blades of grass have lots of chlorophyll (KLAWR-o-fil) in them. Chlorophyll is a chemical that works with the sun to help plants grow.

Sunlight looks white, but it's really made up of many colors. How those colors reflect light is what makes the colors we see. Chlorophyll is especially good at reflecting green light. So that's what we see when we look at grass—green!

AAH, I LOVE THE SMELL OF LEAVES.

WHY DO SOME LEAVES CHANGE COLOR?

Trees rest through winter. Since chlorophyll is no longer needed to make food, it disappears from leaves. Colder nights turn them yellow and orange and red.

POWER OF THREE

Three pigments (natural chemicals made by leaves) that color leaves are chlorophyll (green), anthocyanin (red), and carotenoid (yellow, orange, and brown).

CHLOROPHYLL PIGMENT

ANTHOCYANIN PIGMENT

CAROTENOID PIGMENT

GROWING BIG!

When water freezes, it takes up more room than when it was water.

HOW DOES WATER TURN TO ICE?

GETTING COLD!
Salty ocean water freezes at a lower temperature than freshwater.

Water is made up of teeny tiny chemical bits, called molecules (MOL-uh-kyoolz), that are too small to see. As the molecules get colder, they move more slowly and connect (as if they are hooking onto each other). If the temperature drops to 32 degrees Fahrenheit (or 0°C), they lock stiffly into place in tiny hexagon patterns. That is how ice forms.

ICE IS NICE... IF YOU'RE A PENGUIN!

99

WHAT CAUSES AN EARTHQUAKE?

Gigantic plates of rock lie under Earth's surface. The places where their edges meet are called faults. Sometimes the plates move in different directions, grinding against each other and shaking the area around the fault line. These are earthquakes.

I THOUGHT EARTHQUAKES WERE CAUSED BY PIG STAMPEDES!

CAN EARTHQUAKES HAPPEN UNDERWATER?

Yes. Sometimes earthquakes happen on the bottom of the ocean. They can cause giant, dangerous ocean waves, called tsunamis (soo-NA-meez).

HOW DO WE MEASURE AN EARTHQUAKE?

An instrument called a seismograph (SIZE-ma-graff) measures the energy waves pulsing out from a quake's epicenter (where the quake began) and how long they last.

GUESS NOT.

FAULT LINE

WHAT MAKES TIDES?

Ocean tides—the rising and falling of the water—happen because, as the Earth turns, the gravitational pulls of the moon and sun make the water bulge toward them.

LET'S GO SURFING!

WHY IS OCEAN WATER SALTY?

COWABUNGA, DUDE!

Earth's oceans are very, very old, and very salty. Most of the salt in them comes from land. That's because rain and rivers wash over rocks and carry salty minerals from them to ocean water. More salty minerals reach the ocean from underwater volcanoes and even from falling rain.

WATER, WATER EVERYWHERE

Oceans make up 97 percent of all water on our planet. But people cannot drink ocean water unless the salt is removed.

DESALINIZATION PLANT

103

WHY DOES THUNDER FOLLOW LIGHTNING?

Crashes of thunder are caused by flashes of lightning. When a fiery lightning bolt forks through the sky, it heats up the air around it very quickly. When air gets hot, it expands. And when it gets hot quickly, it has to expand RIGHT NOW. That makes sound waves rip through the air explosively FAST, causing those familiar loud rumbles and BOOMS.

WHEN BOMB'S HUNGRY, HIS TUMMY SOUNDS LIKE THUNDER!

1... 2... 3 ...

When you see lightning, start counting. The number of seconds between a lightning flash and the thunder that follows tells you how far away it is. Each second adds around 1,000 feet (300 m).

INCOMING!

If you're outdoors and can hear thunder, quickly head inside. You're in the lightning danger zone, even if a storm hasn't yet arrived or has already passed.

HEY!

WHAT CAUSES A TORNADO?

Thunderstorms are created when warm, moist air meets cooler, dry air. Certain conditions can cause these air masses to begin swirling around each other and form a tornado. A tornado is a whirling column of air reaching from thunderstorm clouds in the sky down to the ground. Tornado winds spin at up to 300 miles an hour (483 km/h). They can destroy buildings, uproot trees, and throw heavy cars and trucks like toys. Tornadoes can happen any time of year.

HURRICANE KATRINA

SUPERSTORMS!

Cyclone, hurricane, and typhoon are different names for the same weather event—large, swirling storm systems that begin over oceans and seas. Most happen from early June through late November. Rather than roar through quickly like tornadoes, these monster storms last for hours or days.

HURRICANE WILMA

WHAT MAKES A RAINBOW?

Sunlight is made up of many colors. They just remain invisible until right before or after it rains. That's when the air is filled with tiny water droplets. When sunlight hits those droplets, they separate the light into its true colors, and we're treated to stripes of red, orange, yellow, green, blue, indigo, and violet—a rainbow!

AT THE END OF THE RAINBOW IS A POT OF BIRDSEED!

SEEING DOUBLE!

Sometimes raindrops reflect sunlight twice. This makes a double rainbow. The second one has its colors upside down.

WHAT'S IN A NAME?

It's easy to remember the order of a rainbow's colors by thinking of their first letters as a man's name: ROY G. BIV.

I HEARD THAT A COW ONCE JUMPED OVER THE MOON.

A COW?! GET ME A SLINGSHOT! I'M GOING FOR IT!

ROUND AND ROUND IT GOES

The moon orbits (goes around) the Earth every 27.3 days.

WHY CAN WE SOMETIMES SEE THE MOON IN THE DAYTIME?

After the sun, the moon is the brightest thing in the sky. But the moon is only bright because it's reflecting sunlight. As it orbits Earth, it can be seen anytime it is above the horizon (where land and sky seem to meet). Usually, though, the sun is so bright that we don't notice or can't see the moon.

MOON SHADOWS

Unlike the sun, the moon appears to change size. These changes are called phases. As the moon orbits Earth, each night its shape grows until it's a big round circle (a cycle called **waxing**), and then it shrinks back down until it disappears (a cycle called **waning**).

When it looks like a big round ball, it's a **full moon**.

If it's a full circle but not quite, it's called a **gibbous moon**.

When it's a thin sliver, it's called a **crescent moon**.

And when there's no visible moon at all, it's called a **new moon**.

FALLING STARS

Sometimes, "falling stars" streak across the night sky. They aren't stars—they're really small bits of dust or rock called meteoroids. As they enter Earth's atmosphere, they burn up, showing off a fiery trail!

WHY DO STARS TWINKLE?

Stars are far from Earth. Their light waves travel millions of miles before they reach our eyes. All along the way, the waves pass through tiny particles and space gases. That makes starlight look twinkly to those of us on Earth.

SHHH. I'M WISHING ON A STAR...DEAR STAR, PLEASE ZAP SOME PIGS!

STAR LIGHT, STAR BRIGHT?

In the night sky, planets look a lot like stars with one big exception: They don't twinkle. They're closer to Earth, so their light waves don't travel through so much space "stuff."

113

QUIZ TIME

I. People wear special clothing to keep them warm in winter. Match each item with the part of the body for which it's designed. Which item pictured below goes on your head? Your hands? Your feet?

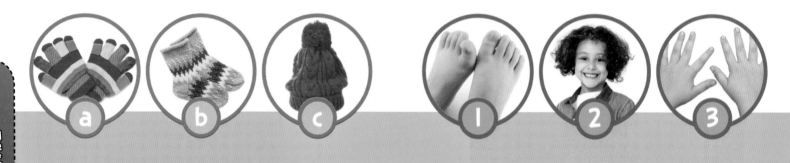

2. People around the world live in different kinds of houses. Which halves below match?

116

3. Six turtles played in the creek. Two swam away. How many are left?

 -  = **?**

4. Use your finger to help this cat find its way through the park and back home.

QUIZ TIME

5. Can you unscramble these crayon color words?

a. lube   b. dre   c. enegr   d. oylewl   e. lupper

6. You want to join a rock band. Point to the invention you might need.

 a
 b
 c
 d

7. Airplanes come in different sizes. Point to the airplane below that could carry the most people. Which could hold only a few people?

 a
 b
 c

8. Which two kinds of fuel pictured below might power a steam train?

a. a pile of wood

b. a pile of bricks

c. a pile of coal

9. Here are some weather words. Can you say which letters are missing from each one?

a. torna_o

b. thu_der

c. hurri_ane

d. ligh_ning

10. Which two of the leaves below might belong to the same tree? How are those two leaves alike? How are they different?

a

b

c

BONUS ACTIVITIES

Chapter 1: Puzzling People

Dress-up relay
(race)

Birds don't wear clothes, but people do! This group game is easy and fun. Line up in two teams. At the opposite end of the room, make two equal piles of too-big clothes and accessories (one for each team). When someone says go, the first player from each team runs down and puts on all of the clothes from her team's pile, then runs back and takes them all off again. The next player in line puts them on, then runs to the other end of the room, takes them off, leaves them in a pile, then runs back to tag the next player. Keep going until every player on both teams has taken a turn. The first team to finish, wins.

Dance
(exercise)

Music can make a person want to dance. Play your favorite kind of music and create your very own dance. You can jump and jiggle, whirl and twirl, dip and glide, or step-step-stomp. Just have fun with it. Maybe somebody else will want to learn your moves!

Chomp
(measuring)

As our jaws grow, our baby teeth are gradually replaced by adult teeth. How much bigger will your jaw grow? Bite into a slice of bread. Use a ruler to measure across the widest part of your bite. Now have a parent or other adult bite into a slice of bread. Measure across his bite to see how much growing you still have to do!

Read and rest
(relaxation)

Reading for only six minutes is said to relax a person. Try it! The next time you're upset, set a timer, then sit down and read for six minutes. (If you cannot read yet, look at a picture book and imagine what's happening in the story.) How do you feel after six minutes?

Chapter 2: Amazing Animals

An eggs-cellent match
(matching)

Different-size birds lay different-size eggs. On two index cards, draw two eggs about the same size and color them the same. Make six or eight more egg pairs. Mix them up and place them facedown, then try to match sets.

Clap a pattern
(concentration)

Each species of firefly has its own flash pattern. Have an adult clap out a simple pattern of three claps. Listen carefully. Can you repeat it exactly? Have her add two or three more claps to the end of her pattern. She can add quick claps or slow claps. How many times can you follow the pattern before messing it up? Take turns being the clapper and the one who repeats.

Wandering web
(balance)

Spiders know how to walk on their own webs without getting stuck—very carefully! Make yourself a web by laying a long piece of string or yarn on the floor in a large circular or crazy mixed-up pattern. Keeping your feet on the string, walk along it on your tiptoes and see how far you can go before losing your balance and falling off your web.

Hibernation station
(deduction)

Bears spend the winter months hibernating. That's a lot of sleep! How long do you sleep each night? Make a chart marked with the seven days of the week. Write down how many hours you sleep each of those nights. Draw a smiley face on the mornings you feel happy when you wake up. Draw a grouchy face on the mornings you feel grumpy. Did you find that how much time you slept made a difference in how you felt in the morning?

Chapter 3: Astounding Inventions

Paper cup telephone
(craft)

Telephones used to rely on how sound traveled through wires. To see this, you can make a simple, old-fashioned phone with two plastic cups (or soup cans) and a long piece of string (kite string works great). First punch a tiny hole in the bottom of each cup. Then thread one end of the string through one cup and the other end through the second cup. Tie knots in the string ends so they won't pull out. (Tip: You can tie each end around a broken toothpick if it won't stay put.) Have a friend hold one cup while you hold the other. Step back until the string is tight. Hold your cup tight against your ear and have your friend talk into his cup. His voice will make the bottom of his cup vibrate. Those vibrations will travel through the string and cause the bottom of your cup to vibrate—and you'll hear what he's saying through your cup.

Beep-bloop
(communication)

The first video games didn't have very exciting sound effects. Using only beeps and bloops, can you make sound effects that would let a player know when they've won a game? Lost a game? Does your voice go up or down to let a player know they've won?

Up, up, and away
(art)

On a piece of paper, draw a hot-air balloon with a square basket underneath. Draw lines to connect the basket to the balloon. Color the basket brown. Draw colorful shapes—circles, squares, and triangles—on the balloon.

BONUS ACTIVITIES

Chapter 4:
Terrific Travel

Circus train
(storytelling)

Make up a story. Pretend you're the engineer on a train filled with circus animals. What if the train broke down and you had to wait hours for repair? What would you do to keep all those restless animals happy? What if they were hungry? What if they escaped?!

Color check
(observation)

School buses are a bright yellow-orange color because that color is supposed to be easiest to see, even in a person's peripheral (side) vision. Test it yourself. On index cards, draw and fill in colored circles (one color/circle per card). Make the colors bright, and create one each of blue, green, yellow, orange, red, black, purple, and brown. Now have somebody hold a color card about one foot out from your ear with the color facing your head. Keep your eyes staring straight ahead as he slowly moves the color card around forward. Raise your hand when you can see what color it is. Which color do YOU see first?

Hello, up there
(observation)

As the International Space Station orbits Earth, it is often visible at night to those of us on the ground. You can find out when it might be passing above your area by checking this NASA website:

spotthestation.nasa.gov/

Float your boat
(experiment)

Buoyancy helps even large ships stay afloat. Test buoyancy by making a flat-bottomed boat out of aluminum foil, making sure the sides are of equal height. Fill a sink about halfway full of water, then float your boat. Drop pennies into your boat, one at time. How many pennies can your boat hold before sinking? Now reshape your boat, giving it a narrower bottom, but refolding its sides so they stay about the same height as before. How many pennies can this boat hold without sinking? Did you think the size of the boat's bottom made a difference?

For some tips and tricks to build your boat, visit these websites:

pbskids.org/zoom/activities/sci/boatsafloat.html

usafa.edu/df/dfe/dfer/centers/stem/docs/AluminumFoilBoats.pdf

Chapter 5:
Nuts About Nature

Freeze tag
(game)

When water molecules get really, really cold, they stop moving. Play freeze tag with your family or a group of friends. Whoever is "it" chases everybody else. When the "it" person touches another player, that person has to stand unmoving, as if frozen, until another "not it" teammate crawls through her legs to unfreeze her. The game is over when every player is frozen.

Salty water
(experiment)

Objects float better in salt water than freshwater. You can see for yourself by pouring regular water into a tall glass until it's about half full. Carefully lower an egg into the glass (make sure the egg is NOT hard-boiled). Does it float or sink? Use a spoon to remove the egg. Stir in six tablespoons (or more) of salt. Again, gently lower the egg into the water. Does it sink or float?

Tornado in a jar
(observation)

Tornadoes form when warm and cold air collide in the sky and begin spinning around one another. You can create your own water "tornado." Fill an empty jar—like a pickle jar—with water, leaving about half an inch at the top. Squirt in plenty of dish-washing liquid. Put the lid on tight, then swirl the jar in a circular motion. Set it down and watch a tornado form.

Night sky puzzle
(craft)

On a dark piece of construction paper, use white and yellow crayons to draw a moon and lots of stars. Color them in. Then glue or paste your picture to the cardboard from an empty cereal box. When it dries, cut it into six or more pieces to create a puzzle, then have fun putting it back together again.

Make a rainbow
(observation)

Rainbows are formed when sunlight hits water droplets at the right angle. On a sunny day, you can make your own rainbow with nothing but a garden hose. Turn on the faucet, then stand with the hose so that the sun is shining behind you and you can see your shadow in front of you. If your hose doesn't have a sprayer on the end, use your thumb to make it spray. Shoot a fine mist of the water into the air, moving it slowly back and forth until you see a rainbow. The water from the hose does the same thing the rain does to make a rainbow in the sky—it refracts the beams of sunlight so that they separate into their different colors.

GLOSSARY

ABDOMEN
an animal's belly

AMPHIBIANS
cold-blooded animals such as frogs and toads, newts, and salamanders that live part of their lives underwater and part on land

ANTENNA
rod or wire or dish-shaped device used to send or receive radio or TV signals

ATMOSPHERE
protective layer of gases surrounding a planet

BUOYANCY
ability to float in water or other liquid

CHAMBER
room

CHARCOAL
hard black material formed when wood or bone is heated without air

DIAPHRAGM
a dome-shaped muscle that stretches across the top of the abdomen; helps people to breathe

EARTHQUAKE
a sudden shaking of the ground

EMBRYO
a developing offspring, still unborn

EMOTION
a feeling, mood, or overall state of mind

EXPERIMENTAL
new, untested

GRAVITATIONAL
a force that causes one object to be attracted to another

HEXAGON
a shape with six straight sides

HOVER
to fly in place, without moving in any direction

LABORATORY
place set up for scientific experiments

MAMMALS
warm-blooded animals with hair or fur that produce milk to nourish their young. Humans are also mammals.

MELANIN
dark, natural coloring in human hair, skin, and the iris of the eye

MINERALS
tiny bits of natural materials, as from rocks

MOLECULES
teeny, tiny chemical bits too small for human eyes to see

ORGANISMS
living things like animals, plants, and people

PREDATORS
animals that hunt others for food

PREY
an animal that is hunted by another for food

RECHARGEABLE (BATTERIES)
able to use electricity to repower after running down

REPTILES
cold-blooded animals, including alligators and crocodiles, lizards and snakes, turtles and tortoises

SATELLITE
a machine put into space to orbit Earth; used to collect information or for communication

TERMITES
small, antlike insects that eat wood

TORNADO
a giant storm with fast-moving winds swirling in a column

ULTRAVIOLET LIGHT/ RAYS
invisible light that comes from the sun

125

INDEX

Boldface indicates illustrations.

A

Airplanes **90-91**, 91, **118**
Alligators **36-37**, 125
Apartment buildings 22, **23**
Archimedes 68
Armadillos **38**, 39
Astronauts 92, 93

B

Baby teeth 18, 120
Balloons 64, **64-65**, 65
Bats 48, **48**, 52, **52-53**, 53
Batteries 84, 87, 125
Bears 48, **48-49**, 121
Birds
    ability to fly 24
    babies 34, **34-35**
    eggs 35, **35**
    feathers 24, **24**, 34
Blue whales 57, **57**
Board games 66, **66-67**, 67
Boats **82-83**, 83, 122
Bones 24, **25**
Burps 20

C

Camouflage 54, 55
Cars 86, **86-87**, 87, 106
Cats
    hair balls 44
    hiccups 21
    landing on feet 44
    licking fur 44, **44-45**
    purring 45
Cave paintings 61, **61**
Cell phones 74, **76-77**, 77
Charcoal 18, 60, 124
Checkers (game) 67, **67**
Cheetahs 56, **56**
Chimpanzees 56, **56-57**
Chipmunks 48, **48**
Chlorophyll 96, 97
Clothing 10, **10-11**, 116, **116**, 120
Cob houses 23, **23**
Cooper, Martin **76-77**, 77
Crayons 60, **60-61**
Crowns 16, **16**

D

Desert horned lizards 55, **55**
Diaphragm 21, 124

E

Earthquakes 100, **100-101**, 101, 124
Echidnas 37, **37**
Echolocation 52, 53
Eggs 35, **35**, 36, **36-37**, 120, 123
Elephants 46, **46-47**, 47, 56, 57
Elevators 68, **68-69**
Elizabeth II, Queen 16, **16**
Eyeglasses 14, **14-15**, 62

F

Fault lines 100, **101**
Fingernails **26-27**, 27
Fireflies 40, **40-41**, 41, 120
Ford, Henry 87
Freckles 13, **13**
Frogs 40, 48, **54-55**, 124
Fruit flies 92, **92**

G

Giraffes 32, **33**, 50, **50-51**
Grass 96, **96-97**
Guitars, electric **72-73**, 73

H

Helicopters 88, **88-89**, 89
Helium balloons 64, **64**
Hibernation 48, 121
Hiccups 21
Higinbotham, William 74
Hot-air balloons **64-65**, 65
Houses, types of 22, **22-23**, 168
Hurricanes 106, **106**

I

Ice **98-99**, 99
International Space Station 92, **92-93**, 122

J

Jansen, Zacharias 62
Jewelry 16, **16-17**

K

Keratin 27
Keytar 73, **73**

L

Leaves 96, **96**, 97, **97**, 119
Lightning **94-95**, 104, **104-105**, 105

M

Melanin 13, 124
Meteoroids 112, **112**
Microscopes 62, **62-63**
Model T (car) 87, **87**
Moon 102, **110-111**, 111
Music 28, 29, 73, 120

O

Ocean water 99, 103

P

Pigments 97, **97**
Pixels 70, **70**
Planets 113, **113**
Platypuses 36, **36**
Poison dart frog **54-55**
Pong (video game) 74, **74**
Porcupines 39, **39**

R

Rainbows 108, **108-109**, 109, 123
Rats 21, **21**
Reading **30-31**, 31, 120
Rickenbacker, Adolf 73

S

Salt 103, 123
Satellites 70, **71**, 125
School buses 80, **80-81**, 81, 122
Seismographs 101, **101**
Senet (game) **66-67**, 67
Ships 83, **83**, 122
Skeletons 24
Skin colors **12-13**, 13
Space Invaders (video game) 74, **74**
Spiders 32, 36, 40, **42-43**, 43, 121
Star Trek (TV show) 77, **77**

Stars 112, **112-113**, 113
Stone Age clothes 10, **10**
Sunburn 13
Sunglasses 14, **14**
Sunlight 96, 108, 111, 123
Superstorms 106

T

Teeth
    baby teeth 18, 120
    brushing 18, **18**
    cavities 18
Telescopes 62, **62**
Television
    cameras 70, **70-71**
    signals 70, 124
Termites 29, **29**, 125
Thunder 104, 105
Tigers 54, **54**
Toenails 27, **27**
Togas 11, **11**
Toothpaste 18
Tornadoes 106, **106-107**, 123, 125
Trains 84, **84-85**, 85, 119, 122
Tsunamis 100, **100**
Turtles **38-39**, 39, 125

U

Ultraviolet light 13, 14, 125

V

Video games 74, **74-75**, 121
Voice box 21

W

Waves 100, **100**, **102-103**
Whales 53, 56, 57, **57**
Winter
    hibernation 48, 121
    special clothing 116, **116**

Y

Yurt **22-23**

PHOTO CREDITS

Staff for This Book
Erica Green, Senior Editor
Amy Briggs, Project Editor
Eva Absher-Schantz, Art Director
Dawn Ripple McFadin, Designer
Lori Epstein, Senior Photo Editor
Annette Kiesow, Photo Editor
Paige Towler, Editorial Assistant
Sanjida Rashid, Design Production Assistant
Michael Cassady, Rights Clearance Specialist
Grace Hill, Managing Editor
Joan Gossett, Senior Production Editor
Lewis R. Bassford, Production Manager
Rachel Faulise, Manager, Production Services
Susan Borke, Legal and Business Affairs

Published by the National Geographic Society
Gary E. Knell, President and CEO
John M. Fahey, Chairman of the Board
Melina Gerosa Bellows, Chief Education Officer
Declan Moore, Chief Media Officer
Hector Sierra, Senior Vice President and General Manager,
    Book Division

Senior Management Team, Kids Publishing and Media
Nancy Laties Feresten, Senior Vice President; Jennifer
Emmett, Vice President, Editorial Director, Kids Books;
Julie Vosburgh Agnone, Vice President, Editorial
Operations; Rachel Buchholz, Editor and Vice President,
NG Kids magazine; Michelle Sullivan, Vice President, Kids
Digital; Eva Absher-Schantz, Design Director; Jay Sumner,
Photo Director; Hannah August, Marketing Director;
R. Gary Colbert, Production Director

Digital Anne McCormack, Director; Laura Goertzel, Sara
Zeglin, Producers; Jed Winer, Special Projects Assistant;
Emma Rigney, Creative Producer; Brian Ford, Video
Producer; Bianca Bowman, Assistant Producer; Natalie
Jones, Senior Product Manager

ROVIO ENTERTAINMENT LTD.
Pekka Laine, Project Editor
Mari Elomäki, Project Editor
Anna Makkonen, Graphic Designer
Jean Michel Boesch, Comic Artist